IN ANOTHER LIFE

Selected Poems
Jeff Arnett

My dear Sir Tru –
The first copy goes
to you for without your
faith and wit, I would
still be bookless.
My gratitude.
Your liege,

"Whoever you are, now I place my hand
upon you, that you be my poem."

From "To You"

—Walt Whitman

For my wife Patricia and daughter Miranda

Cover design and artwork by Jeff Arnett
Graphics by Olwen Bruce
Printed by Community Printers
Santa Cruz, California

Contact Jeff at Instagram: Jeff Arnett@jefffarnett3

Published by Impossible Books,
San Francisco
& 12 Gates to the City Press
Santa Cruz, California

ISBN: 979-8-218-24022-6

Instagram

Web Site

Acknowledgments

To all the poets and writers, many gone but not forgotten, who gifted me in passing, especially Tim Fitzmaurice, mentor, editor, poet, friend.

Stephen Kessler

Myron Greenman

Naomi Clark

Robert Bly

William Stafford

Carolyn Forche

George Hitchcock

Morton Marcus

Lynn Luria Sukenick

Marilyn Krysl

Rhoda Lerman

Jeffrey Deshell

Bridget Klauber

Cassandra Kircher

Tilly Shaw

David Swanger

Gary Young

Charles Atkinson

Paul Skenazy

Don Rothman

Gary Miles

Thad Nodine

Ken Weisner

Roger Bunch

Chris Krohn

Eric Cummins

Patricia Arnett

(my IT girl)

Contents

Abalone shells hung on the walls
"like the ears of the house."

The abalone shells, in one of Jeff Arnett's poems, are ears. For him physical objects are listening for the truth. Often when we write we hide inside our songs and throw metaphorical tarps over the bones of our life at the expense of truth. Sometimes we grapple with life staying true to its complexity. We let it resist being defined, tamed, shaped by us. Jeff listens to the materials. He is a sculptor of stone and life.

There is a familiar, and to me always peculiar, image of the process of sculptors, that says they are carving off the layers of the marble to let the secret truth buried inside the stone emerge. It will do as a metaphor for disclosing but the art and practice seems more complex than that. The stone has more to say about it. People forget that the word Revelation, as in the Biblical Apocalypse, means uncovering, disclosing, unveiling, revealing. But the stone, like the realities of living, cannot be simply metaphor. It is hard truth. It always has its say.

It seems fitting that Jeff Arnett, who spends countless hours each day scraping, scratching, grinding, polishing the surfaces of stone, would create poetry that does the same thing with lives. It scratches at the surface layers, trusting the resistances in it and exploring the openings, the softer gateways in the rock, releasing something true from his own experience. The lives and experiences of his loved family. Jeff and his daughter, his wife, his father and mother, each become part of this statuary hall bristling with life, like animated statues. These poems add animation to the sculptor's work, the work he is already passionately doing when he patiently polishes the stone.

He often finds this stone himself in places where it is otherwise overlooked. I remember the heavy stone we carried one day from an abandoned quarry. We lugged it a half mile and drove it a mile or so to the garage where he works, his home studio.

I chose this large piece of marble for a garden sculpture. "Let's call this one Robinson Jeffers," I said, thinking of the Big Sur poet. The resulting bust looked nothing like Jeffers, but it obeyed the stone and this respectful obedience to what is given, to the fact of the stone, looked everything like Jeffers to me.

I have followed the shaping of this garden, these poems and their artistic obedience to what rings true for Jeff. What is here reflects his love for life and for people and their complexity. The images altered from old photos anchor it for us. We can see that these are real people in these snapshots, often in their most hopeful moments. "Snapshots are a way of delaying extinction"— a friend once wrote. It is right that this hope is embedded in these images. It is what Jeff finds in the stone as well and expresses so lovingly.

Tim Fitzmaurice

The Capital

This was the beginning
of memory for me,
the tall columns still
white in the twilight,
snow falling white
in the darkening,
Lincoln looking very
grave and I remember
why all these years
later I love the feel
of marble smooth
and cool under
my hands.

Shot at the Capital

The Lion's Roar

I remember snow and a sled with red runners,
the lion who roared when I pulled its tail,
a bleeding arm after a fall from a stone wall,
lost in a foreign city searching for a zoo
where the real lions would roar my name
the boy I cannot remember,
his name or who he belonged to.

Dragged into airplanes by strangers
posing as my parents,
crying to be left behind.
When we landed, as we always did,
I ran out of hearing so only a lion—
a real lion—could call me back.

Soon, like all my friends,
I learned to live outside
my body as we ranged farther
and farther from houses,
finding the deserted forest
where only the dead leaves
could tell we were there.
We would drink from the old spring
without fear and the leopard frogs from the lake
we caught and caged, dead within days,
and the box turtles we gathered and penned up
in a corral until the turtle rustlers
from downstream escaped with burlap bags
full of our slow victims of turf wars.

In our free time, we threw mud balls at passing cars,
put up crude roadblocks of logs and stones
at the boundaries of our territory.
On my own, I stole mail from the neighbors
and delivered it unopened to a tree stump

in the deserted forest where no one
could read it.

Later I learned it was not enough
to run down hills in the falling light
chasing shadows into the tall grass.
They wanted more from you
than table manners.
They wanted you to sit still
for hours at a time, days on end
with minutes offered like rations
for good behavior.

They wanted you to wake up and fall asleep
in unison with a room full of strangers.
They wanted you to learn their rules
and act as if you believed in them.
As they taught me how to add and subtract
and multiply and divide, I left my body
behind where it was always waiting for me
when they released me back into my world
that grew smaller and smaller until
I finally deserted the forest and the forest
deserted me and the lion roared no more
and no one called the name
I had yet to learn.

I became their captive
who never roars
but prowls the edges
of a foreign city
where lions are forbidden
and the cages invisible.

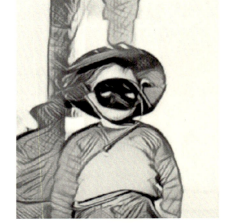

Captive's Disguise

4

I Miss My Hat

I am the faded photograph
wearing a battered hat
frowning at the camera
held by my father
while my brother and sister
furnish the cages for the leopard frogs
we caught along the shores
of Lake Barcroft that morning—
following the creek
we roamed in days almost
beyond remembering
in my Virginia childhood.

My hat still lives
in the fickle closet of memory
and in dog-eared photographs
without negatives or exact dates,
my hat misshapen in that casual way
of felt and time and the contours
of a boyhood spent outside
in the woods of Falls Church
with my brother and the kid next door,
older so wiser who had his hat too.

I wore my hat when we foraged
for leopard frogs and box turtles
to capture, pen and cage
because that's who we were
in the daylight and at night
chasing fireflies in the humid summer
dark to keep in glass jars
till morning when we found
their dead bodies and dumped them
outside before our mothers complained
and so we spent our summer,

my hat and me careless
of everything but the hunt
for innocent creatures to keep

because I was a hunter
with a hat and no idea
I would grow up hatless
staring at this faded photograph.

Cagey Frogs

Box Scores

Studying the familiar table
of at bats and hits, runs and rbi's,
walks and strikeouts,
a code of childhood, searching
for Mickey Mantle's line
back in the fifties when
I was a center fielder
for the Billy Mitchell Bombers
in San Antonio, Texas with my red hat
and black high-top tennis shoes
because back then no one
had spikes in little league.

You had a glove and a favorite
player, all you needed
to dream big or at least
dream of being in center
field when a high fly fell
into your glove as you raced
back to the fence at full speed
with all your friends watching
and your parents in the stands
happy at last you are their son.

In Uniform

A Man, I Imagine

Impossible to decipher this strange
alphabet of longing he left
to remind me to study the fireflies
at night, take out the trash
in the morning, tend
his flock of ghosts.

I barely recognize the words,
as if he made up a language of ciphers
to confuse me, marking his disappearance
with these faint imprints on the curling
paper left in the far corners
of his abandoned house deep
in the forest where he lived
a life of simple comings and
goings from here and there
without leaving a trace
that he'd been anywhere.

Maybe his existence
is no more real than these
signs he left behind, words
I cannot understand, or
perhaps he was not ever here
in this poem or even alive
before it was written and so
the mystery of the strange
man is no mystery at all
but a small toy I use
to pass the time
and puzzle the clues
of his passing with
barely a glance
in my direction.

Secret Garden

My father lives in a secret
garden where the sun sings
to him about the stars
and the dark galaxies
where no suns sing
to the dead sent there
to dream of the evil
they left behind
in the eyes of the children
they bore into the light
of the sun that does not shine
while my father sings
in his garden of secrets

singing the song of his
father who died when
he was young, a song
of dark corners where
the light does not touch
the shrinking heart
of a little boy who lives
without the song of his
father banished
to a far galaxy
of the heart
where he sings
his garden of secrets.

Father in War

From my father's notebooks during World War II

From Paramoribo, Dutch Guiana
to Belem, Brazil where you noted:
"Have dinner by 6:30, 1/2 hour lunch.
Get some exercise."
I never asked what you did
during the war, the good war.

In your little blue notebook,
embossed with the title,
"PERMANENT RECORD
AND MEMORANDUM,"
you wrote, "Tact & diplomacy
in dealing with Brazilians.
Remember, it's their country
and they are not at war."
Tact & diplomacy--
these you brought home
from the war.

Sometimes your writing is so small
and faint—in pencil—I need
a magnifying glass to read it.
"Plan for 500 each at Natal
& Belem. 300 at Recife."
500 what?
"There will be a cargo section
in the ferrying command."
Your own shorthand. Military speak.
Growing up around it
I never really learned the language.

"Air Mail from States pretty good service
6¢ - 1/2 oz. Boat mail service poor.

5% of officer's mail is censored.
25-30% of enlisted men's. . . .
No reference to location. . . .
or activities of troops."
Somehow this explains why
you were an officer—that
and tact & diplomacy.

"Get white uniform in Georgetown."
When did you wear white in wartime?
Brazil and tropical nights
of dark rum and native women?
It doesn't sound like you,
though tact & diplomacy
can take you places . . .

"Need for pistols by personnel
in Brazil . . . 75 in Natal
have none . . . Importance
of little things in indicating discipline-
belt buckles, etc. . . . Value
of blackboards in keeping track
of operations . . . Importance
of pleasant conditions for flying
personnel . . . a good meal,
hot coffee, magazines, etc."
I wonder about the "etceteras,"
the little details of discipline,
who you really were outside
the cramped notes of this tiny
permanent record and memorandum.

Sprinkled with homilies:
"A leader is one who inspires
people, not one who waits
to see what course will be popular."
Did you teach me this?

Did you use these in speeches
to the troops?
Did you have any troops?

And then the mysterious
"Whistling frogs of Piaico . . .
Drivers in Georgetown . . .
Belem - riot of color on houses -
Col. Pinto - Brazilians very gracious
and cooperative . . .
Green wood at Belem, straw mattresses."
Almost poetry emerging
from the tiny book.

Followed by page after page
of departures and arrivals—
Belem, Fortalezo, Natal, Recife,
Barbados, Bahia, Ascension, Rio—
flying back and forth, again and again.
I could find these places on a map
but I have no idea what you did
to make the world safe for democracy.

Later you write, "When a thing ceases
to grow it begins to die," followed by
a brief story of King Midas—
I can barely read the words—
"who was captured by the trick
of mixing wine with the water
of the fountain where the gods drank."
I don't remember you telling me
how to keep growing to avoid dying
or how to know the father faintly
alive in these fading glimpses
but I've used your notebooks
for my own lists—errands,
groceries, expenses, notes

on The Aesthetics of Lust,
a story never finished.

Gathering these fragments—
a son's timid archaeology—
I remember I have small hands,
like you, and how little they hold,
your cramped notebooks the clues
to a father still alive in a country
where they speak a language
of silence and ciphers.

In Uniform

Finding Him

The moon flares through
the smudged windows
of the forgotten house
and the familiar carping
of God or some trick
of light spreads
across the rough wooden
floor as my father lies
dying at the foot
of my bed.

I came here to listen
to the old man's
forgotten hymns,
to feel the touch
of his psalms,
to hold his dying
song in my heart.

But it could be just
the wind chafing
against the thin walls
or the moonlight
cringing on the floor.

If the moon is great
and I am small
why should I be
left alone in my
grief at finding
nothing here
I can call
my own?

Late Summer

*"He look'd in years, yet in his years were seen
A youthful vigor, and autumnal green"*

—John Dryden

The late summer green
recedes into the shadow
of the long days of lightning bugs,
leopard frogs, box turtles and strange
faces of family and friends, dead and alive.

Harvester of sunlight,
the moss between the cracks
in my life is green with memory
clinging to the droplets of sun.
No rain but the mist is thick
with the flicker of fireflies
and a boyhood spent searching
for my father who traveled
around the world who knows
why, reason has nothing to do
with it but now I am reasonable
when then I was chasing fireflies
and had no time to worry about
who would tuck me into bed, did
anyone or was it the black maid
in Alabama whose dark arms
held me while my mother drank
her bourbon and water?
And my father traveled who knows
where for god and country or
because men do what they have to do
and sometimes not much else.

A Father's Forest

In this gallery of shadows,
the stillness of dark rhymes
in a boyhood forest
where my father is buried.
In the shadow's stillness,
running through the forest,
he is sadder than a child should be
searching for his father
who left him long before
I distilled self-pity with rum.

The image is here,
in the dimness of age,
not boxed or mounted or
recorded except in black
and white without shadows
unless my father's laughter or
the whisper of his bare feet
over the fallen leaves
of a forest I know
does not exist except
in the still life of memory
where my father is buried
—no one can tell me where.

Still Life

Priest of Hands

I have written before
of my ageless mother
as she enters my dreams
but tonight I am going
home humbled
by the priest of hands.

The train moves so quickly
I am never certain
if my mother is ill
or dying from the wafers
of darkness they serve.

I can see the shadows
cast by the tall trees,
the train windows
flinching as night falls.

The ghostly conductor
frisks me for light
but I have nothing
to give him so we hum
together, my mother
swaying with the grim
breathing of the train,
the priest of hands
consoling us and death
flying above the tall trees,
spires of the dark
church and my mother
gently blessed
in praying sleep.

Burial At Sea

1.
My hand, surprised by the grit
of the bone, nestled in the fine
sediment your body has become.
Do I shake the box, like breakfast
cereal, spreading you over
this mourning sea?

Instead, I pull handfuls of you
from the little gold box
(so small and tidy)
and toss you to the wind,
into the blue Pacific waters.
Your ash coats the oil of my palms
and I want to keep it there,
but there are strangers in the boat
so I wipe my hand on my thighs
and feel the grit of bone rub
against my dark skin.

With the wide blue sea
to receive you
and the sun banking
the clouds at last,
I let my hands drag
in the wake of the boat
so I can finally leave
you in peace.

Long before the sea

2.
What was it you wanted
to say to me that last night
before you died?
Were you grateful for the garden
of orchids we planted
that never bloomed?
For you I planted the black bamboo
bearing sour fruit, only one,
pale and wrinkled.
You muttered, "There is life in the forest."
But you could barely turn your head.
I forgot a lifetime of questions.

3.
In the dream I see you pulling weeds
in the tropic sun, dark and bent,
beyond you a young boy runs
into a bamboo forest and I recall the words
I found on the bathroom mirror this morning,
carefully printed with red nail polish on the old glass:
"When you comfort one you do not love,
a refrigerator hums in your heart."
Another mystery for your children.

There are ghosts beneath this tumorous moon
who multiply in this region of water shadows.
And there are other alarms you did not sound.
With a congenital deformity of the heart
I struggle to breathe in the shadows.

4.
I am older now than
I have ever been
since we gave you up
to the dolphins, the green
sea turtles and the strand

of rainbows, the blue
jasmine water taking
you out to sea.

All the other mourners
wore dark glasses while
the boat rocked us to and fro.

Back on land I weed ghosts
in your black bamboo forest,
no sign of the sea except
an occasional sea gull.
You know nothing of my life.

I dream of you dreaming
in the belly of a black ferry
itself dreaming in the hold
of a black ferry to frighten
away the silence.

Before the Sea

The Anatomy of Silence

During much of my life,
my heart has been stopped
explaining all those fearful pauses.
Like the time I held her in my arms
and could not pronounce the word love.
Or the time my father died
and I could not feel the knobs to doors,
the handles of drawers,
the steering wheel of my car.

And finally it explains
when I kissed my mother
for the last time,
in the vast silence of her dying,
I could hear her heartbeat
for the first time.

Heartbeat

Night Ferry

When I arrive at the dock
the ferryman tells me,
"In the next life you will be
a handful of sand."

Crossing the lake
we follow the moon
lapping at the water.
"I want wise words to be spoken,"
the ferryman calls
to no one in particular
but I am the only passenger.

I sit near the stern ferryman
who grips the tiller of moonlight
as we watch dreams rise
and disappear
in the ferry's wake.

"I have taken this journey
a thousand times," he says,
"but I don't remember you
or your pale friend."
I look behind me and recognize
my grandfather who died
when I was born, smiling
at me, the moonlight
glinting off his gold tooth.

He says nothing but gestures
for me to follow him to the bow
where my father, dead
these thirty years, holds
the railing and stares
at the moon where
our prayers wait
to answer us.

We say nothing but our hands
touch his on the cold railing
as the night ferries us
toward the far shore
and the waiting moon.

Journey Men

Soft Calypso

The barkless days are hidebound,
bleak tokens of vows gone astray.
It does no good to echo
their silent yowls. The flood
of names—silent,
remorseless, begging me
to listen to the curse of water.

Quibbling with the elements,
I squat at the wall with the rest
as we lower buckets to a mirror
surrounded by toads: one after
the other they unravel
their tongues spliced
with dreams of rain.

At night my father forgets
his lightless eyes at the pain
of seeing me for the last time.
I leave a bilateral imprint in his heart.
We pretend to cross ourselves
but the river is too wide.

The silt of old wounds coats
our feet so we begin
a soft calypso on the shore,
finally holding hands.
Without asking, my father
begins to laugh and without
thinking I join him.

Before Shadows

A Father's Promise

Above us the sandstone cliffs
darken and the blood thins
with the promise of a cold winter.
Black terns stalk the shoreline
as my father waits for me
on the little dock where we
used to fish for white bass.

My father joins his shadow
hand to mine over the water,
our hands rippling
as the lake darkens.

Back in our beds
when we finally fall sleep
the children will sleep too.
I should visit them at night
with blankets and food
but I am afraid my father
will disappear if I leave him
alone and childless.

My father has promised
not to leave me but I see
distance in his eyes
so I follow him to the shore
without looking back,
feel his grip loosen
as we walk into the dark
lake as the echo
of his dying murmurs
on the far shore.

The Names of Trees

Walking down a familiar street
I wonder at the names of trees—
sycamore, maple, chestnut—
pass a silver-haired woman
in a purple bathrobe,
bent over in her driveway
to pick up the morning paper.

In my hand I hold a chestnut,
worn smooth like the one
among my father's keepsakes
I found after his death.

I don't know why my father kept
a single chestnut but searching
for some object to show my students
there are no ideas but in things,
and if I were to write a poem
for my father, I would write
of the hard brown chestnut
in my hand, but I don't really know
if the tree shading the old woman
is sycamore or maple or if my father
ever knew his father or if he died
before he could give him anything
but the name we share and this chestnut
in my hand because I write this
thirty years after his death forgetting
what he left me or if he left me anything
but love and what is that but an idea,
nothing really but an idea
and this smooth hardness
in my heart that I know
but cannot not name.

Blue Quail

"Glimpses that can make us less forlorn."
—Virgil, Aeneid, III, ll. 90-91

Driving the winding road home,
a child sleeping in the backseat,
I glimpse a quail in the shadows,
blue, I think. Blue quail?

Dusk and the dim mountain road,
my mother and father
follow me in the failing light,
with that ghostly lisp of lessons unlearned.
They will never know their granddaughter
who sleeps over ruts and bumps
blessed with sleep and forgetting.

In the falling light
my parents have become shadows
of regret—my sad father singing "Danny Boy"
in his soft tenor while my mother
dances barefoot and gay
in that careless way of ghosts.

Maybe there are no blue quail
and my father and mother, long dead,
no more here than up there,
yet I saw something blue
in the evening shadows of oak
and madrone, following
the car with its sleeping child,
who will remember nothing
until it's her turn to forget.

Braille Light

Shards and Shreds

"The time has come, the clock says time has come.
Here in the mid-waste of my life I pause,
The hour is in my hand, and in my heart
Miscellany of shards and shreds . . . "
—Conrad Aiken, "Preludes"

Sitting in my car, I see a boat
glint white off the blue lake,
and write, "The white moth
feeds at night," then "The child kicks
at a fish dying in the rain."

Barely visible through sheets of rain,
I watch crows feed in a brown field.
 "A curfew of heartbeats,"
I write. "Bells peal long
enough to escape their sound."

I hear my father's soft tenor
in the church now a roadside rest stop.
I am surrounded by stories
invented by the old men
who die without sons.
At the sound of my father's voice
I look up from the page:

There is no church,
no pealing bells, no father,
no words on the page.
just the markings of time
in braille light.

Ponder Heart

After the transplant
they showed you your heart and lungs,
spread out on a metal tray,
dissected in several pieces
—they were looking for tumors.

 In the Gore Room, the technician
held the pieces of your heart
together in his hands to show
what it looked like before
it was cut from your chest.

You held, touched your heart,
your lungs, the texture of sponges,
thanking them for 33 years
of labored breathing,
but life, saying goodbye.

Your first cardiologist told you
you'd never make it past 30.

They let you take home a sliver
of your old heart
the size of a quarter,
a souvenir
for old times sake.

I offered to bury it in the garden
under a flowering hibiscus
or the tulips that you love.
But you didn't want to let it go yet.
It's in a plastic bag in the freezer.
I know because it fell out last night
when I was looking for ice cream.

In the garden it could feed
the hungry roots of the evening rose
or nourish the creeping thyme.

It must be hard to let go
of even a sliver of the heart
that kept you alive longer
than you dared hope.
Now you have her heart,
the mother of three from Modesto,
a blind woman killed in a crosswalk,
Her seeing eye dog, Cato, uninjured.
A stranger's heart, her lungs,
I wonder, her soul . . .

Now you can walk upstairs
without doubling over
gasping for breath.
Now you can walk up hills,
ride a bike, even run a few steps,
finally keep up with your daughter
because a stranger died
with your blood type,
about your size,
died never seeing
what hit her.

Your life is different now
the sundry drugs to keep
your body from destroying
the stranger's heart, her lungs.
Your new heart pondering
what body is this?

If you let go of the last
of your old heart, then bury it
in the garden under the blood
red rose bush, give your heart
the fullest sun, the finest mulch,
the sweetest water till it becomes
a rich red flower alive with
the mystery we still struggle
to understand.

Heartfelt

31

And the Cow Jumped Over the Moon

5 am—my shift.
I stare at the moon's bright crescent
over the night sea, with this squirming
animal who swallows anything
in this bottle I offer her.

Early enough for bird song,
I listen in my blinking daze
and cannot tell if it's the robins
or the sparrows—wondering
why am I not in my bed
dreaming of sleep.

But I begin to savor
the moon and bird song
and the twinkle, twinkle
of little stars, still half
asleep like this daughter
sucking the bottle dry
in my arms.

The Dish Runs Away With the Moon

We spend our mornings,
rising with her first cries,
believing that the cow
will some day jump
over the laughing dog
while the dish runs away
with the moon
and how I wonder
what you are,
rosy child
bewitching sleep.

How I Wonder Who You Are

Lessons For A Sleeping Daughter

"The Word is sacred to a child."
— N. Scott Momaday, *House Made of Dawn*

In orbit the astronauts can see
the wakes of ships.
On earth red heals
even the broken hearted.
In space the smaller stars
last longer than big stars.

Above your sleeping eyes
the honeybee sees clearly on the wing
but blurry at rest on your nose.

"Triboluminescene"
is the little burst of light
created in your mouth
when your teeth bite
into some gay words.

"Ah" as in father
is common to all languages.
When you awaken
the honeybee will be gone
and the little stars will shine
brighter, says father.

Say "Father"

Speaking Blue

That morning, a man in a suit,
briefcase in one hand,
bagpipes in the other,
walked under the bridge
as I passed over.

The butterfly says blue,
explains my daughter.

The butterfly is really the magenta
blossom of a nearby bougainvillea
but speaking blue becomes a butterfly
and makes perfect sense to a tired father
who remembers nothing of speaking
to flowers as if they could fly
as high as a child's arms trying
to catch the bold butterfly
painting the sky blue.

The man with the briefcase needs
his bagpipes as much as I need
to learn to speak the blue
of flowering butterflies.

The butterfly says blue

Breathing Fingernails

Among her collections of cut hair,
bottle caps, rocks, and marbles,
my daughter collects fingernail
clippings in a round silver box,
a mirror inset in its lid.
They say our fingernails
keep growing after death
even as we lie in a box.

We live at the bottom of an ocean
of air and with every inhalation
we breathe in our ancestors,
all they were, all they became,
every molecule, every atom
of desire, every wisp
of their ghostly fingernails
passing into our lungs,
inhaling their prayers.

My father and mother,
oxygen and carbon now,
elements of our being,
still becoming my daughter's
blood, hair, fingernails.

The air she breathes,
her every breath,
atoms of my parents,
inhaling the deep currents
of ancestors who flow
into this vast sea
of the dead, exhaling
memories so faint
our lungs barely move,
our nostrils barely flare,

the musk of life released
when the last breath
escaped their lips,
every man, every woman
becoming this ocean of air
we breathe day and night,
mingling life and death
in this sacred exchange
between our world and theirs.

Dancing in Air

Clear Sailing

For My Daughter

I read the crumpled list
marked "Confidential,"
a wish list of supplies
for a trip on the boat
you will own some day.

First on the list, "Boat,
emergency food and water:
oars, an extra sail,
compass and astrolabe,
life jacket, 'floaty' toys,
a raft and rubber bands."

 "Learn how to sail a boat,"
you write, "find good boat.
Learn how to use a compass.
Read the stars."

"Find best route & how long,
find where to land."

I have wished for these
all my life but I am still
waiting for the wind
to lift me up and carry
me away from what
I cannot say and you
don't say either
but your list
makes it clear
you plan to leave
with only a letter left
behind explaining why
you sailed away, ending

your list with "plan
for what to do
once we get there."

If you can, teach me
to read the stars too.

Read the Stars

In Another Life

We live in a small shack
made of old planks
from a stranded boat.
The roof and sides we covered
with abalone shells
we found on the shore.
In the summer they reflect
the heat of the sun,
in the winter they catch the rain
like cupped hands,
and all year long
they listen to the wind
like the ears of a rainbow.

We live on the mud flats
of a great river.
Like the grey heron
we hunt for crabs,
frogs and slow fish.

In fair weather
I take the little boat
with no sail and troll
for the fish who live
deeper than a man can dive.
With its crooked finger
my long line lures them
to the land where I
have been stranded
all my life.

You keep the fire burning
in case I should return
with one arched
over by back,

its scales flickering
in the firelight
as I lay it at your feet.
And when we sleep
the ears of the house
listen to the murmur
of our dreams.

For My Father and Mother

About the Author

Jeff Arnett is a poet and sculptor living in Santa Cruz, California with his wife Patricia and his 1960 Metropolitan.

After graduating from UC Santa Cruz with two BAs and a detour in retailing with local stores ID and the BX, he returned to writing with a masters in creative writing at the University of Colorado, Boulder. He taught writing at UCSC for 26 years while trying to maintain his own connection to word and stone. Finally retired, Arnett has the time and passion for creating stone, bronze and wood sculptures. Since becoming involved in Santa Cruz Open Studios ten years ago, he has created over two hundred sculptures and continues to write and publish his poetry.

Contact Jeff: instagram.com/jeffarnett3/

Author with Horn